LAUNCH PAD LIBRARY

MY AMAZING BODY

RACHEL WRIGHT

TWO CAN

In association with
FRANKLIN WATTS

How to use this book

Cross references
Above the heading on the page, you will find a list of subjects in the book which are connected to the topic. Look at these pages to find out more about the subjects.

See for yourself
See for yourself bubbles give you the chance to test out some of the ideas in this book. They explain what you will need and what you have to do to see if an idea really works.

Quiz corner
In the quiz corner, you will find a list of questions. The answers to the quiz questions are somewhere on the two pages. Can you answer all the questions about each topic?

Glossary
Difficult words are explained in the glossary near the back of the book. These words are in **bold** on the page. Look them up in the glossary to find out what they mean.

Index
The index is at the back of the book. It is a list of words about everything mentioned in the book, with page numbers next to the words. The list is in the same order as the alphabet. If you want to find out about a subject, look up the word in the index, then turn to the page number given.

Contents

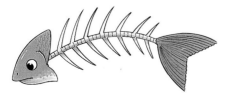

Your amazing body

Your body is an amazing machine. It can move, think, listen and talk. It also mends itself, changes shape and grows. Your body is made of lots of different parts, all working together. You can see some parts, such as your skin and hair. Others, such as your **brain** and **bones,** are hidden inside you.

Before you were born
You started your life inside your mother's tummy. At first you were just a tiny speck, about the size of a full stop. Then you grew and grew, until you were ready to be born.

◀ It takes forty weeks for a baby to grow inside its mother's tummy, then the baby is ready to be born.

Growing up
When you were growing from a baby into a toddler, your body changed quickly. You grew about 20cm a year. You are still growing and changing now, but much more slowly. At seven years old, you grow about 6cm taller each year. When you are a teenager, your body will start to grow and change faster again.

Growing older

Many people stay healthy all through their grown-up years. They take care of their bodies by keeping fit, eating well and taking time to relax.

▼ Older adults often spend time doing the things they enjoy most, such as playing with grandchildren.

▲ As you grow older, your body becomes stronger and you can run faster.

Teenagers

Between the ages of about ten and fourteen, your body will grow taller and change shape. By the time you are about twenty, you will be fully grown.

As girls grow up, they become more rounded, like their mothers. Boys develop broader shoulders and their voices become deeper. Both girls and boys become more hairy as they grow older.

Quiz Corner

- What happens to your body between the ages of ten and fourteen?
- At about what age are you fully grown?
- What happens to a boy's voice as he grows older?
- How can you stay healthy all your life?

5

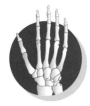

look at: Your muscles, page 8, Breathing, page 12

Your skeleton

Inside your body, there is a strong framework of 206 **bones** called a skeleton. Your skeleton gives your body its shape and strength. If you didn't have a skeleton, you would be as floppy as a bean bag. Your skeleton also helps to protect fragile parts inside your body.

Inside bones

Your bones are not dead and dried up. They are alive, just like the rest of you. Your bones are hard and solid on the outside, but inside many of them have a fatty jelly called bone marrow. Bone marrow helps to make your **blood**.

bone

marrow

CHATTERBOX

Insects and crabs don't have a skeleton inside their bodies. Instead they have a hard outer shell, called an exoskeleton, which protects their soft insides.

▼ Some of the bones in your skeleton are tiny. Others are long and strong.

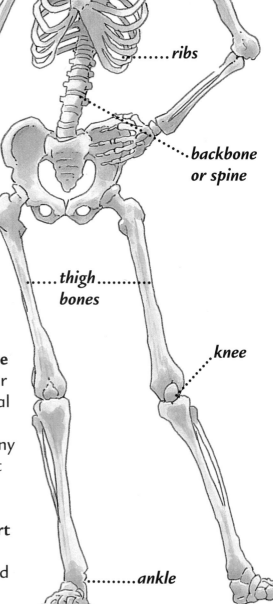

skull

ribs

backbone or spine

thigh bones

knee

ankle

Skull and rib cage
Each bone in your body has a special job to do. Your skull makes a bony helmet to protect your **brain**. Your ribs make a cage around your **heart** and **lungs**, which are soft and could be hurt easily.

Joints

Wherever bones meet in the skeleton, you have a joint. Your knees are hinge joints. They let you move your legs up and down. Your shoulders are ball and socket joints. They let you move your arms in circles.

▲ Your spine is bendy because it is made up of lots of little bones and joints.

Broken bones

If you break a bone, new bone grows to join the broken ends together. A hard bandage called a plaster cast helps to keep the bone straight while it mends.

Quiz Corner

● Which part of your skeleton protects your heart?

● What sort of joints are your hip joints?

● What is another name for your backbone?

▼ You can bend, twist and turn your body because you have joints between your bones.

Finger joints are called knuckles.

Shoulders are ball and socket joints.

Elbows are hinge joints.

Hips are ball and socket joints.

Knees are hinge joints.

Toes have hinge joints.

7

Your muscles

Muscles make your body move. Many of your muscles are fixed to the **bones** of your skeleton by strong straps, called tendons. Every time you run, jump or walk, lots of these muscles pull on your bones. This makes your bones move, which makes your body move.

▼ Your muscles will stay fit and strong if you make them work hard by playing energetic games.

Pairs of muscles

Many of your muscles work in pairs. One muscle pulls a bone one way, then its partner pulls the bone back again.

When you bend your elbow, your biceps muscle becomes shorter, pulling your arm up.

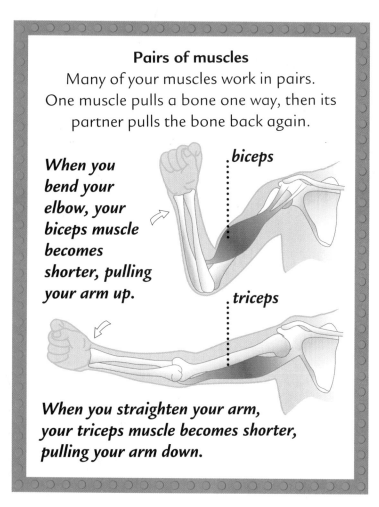

biceps

triceps

When you straighten your arm, your triceps muscle becomes shorter, pulling your arm down.

Sending messages

Your **brain** controls your muscles. It works out which muscles you need to move each part of your body. Your brain sends messages to your muscles to pull on your bones. Then, when your muscles have pulled, they send messages back to your brain.

Pulling faces

Not all your muscles pull on bones. Some of the muscles in your face pull on your skin. You use these muscles every time you smile, frown, or pull a funny face.

▲ Every time you frown, your body uses more than 40 muscles. A smile uses only about 15 muscles. So if you want to save muscle power – smile!

Different muscles

You have three different types of muscle in your body. Each type has a different job to do. One type pulls your bones, to make you move. Another type pushes your food through your body and a third type makes your **heart** beat.

Quiz Corner

● What do muscles help you to do?

● Why are energetic games good for you?

● How many different types of muscles are there in your body?

● Which uses more muscles – a smile or a frown?

9

look at: Blood, page 14, Taking care of yourself, page 28

Eating

Your body needs food to help it grow and work properly. But your body cannot use the food you eat just as it is. Food has to be chewed and chopped up, then changed inside you, until it is small enough to pass into your **blood**. Then your blood can carry it to all the different parts of your body.

Food tubes

Inside your body, there is a long tube which goes from your mouth all the way to your bottom. The top part of this tube is fairly straight, but the bottom part is wiggly. Different things happen to your food as it travels through each part of this tube.

◄ Your body takes all the goodness it needs from your food, then it pushes out the **waste**.

CHATTERBOX

Snakes don't chew their food the way you do. When an egg-eating snake spies a tasty looking egg, it opens its mouth wide and swallows the egg whole.

Healthy eating

You need to eat small amounts of lots of different kinds of foods to give you **energy** and to help you grow. Eggs, meat and fish all help you grow. Bread and pasta give you energy. Fruit and vegetables are full of **vitamins and minerals**.

....When you chew, your teeth chop up your food and your spit makes it soft enough for you to swallow.

... After you swallow, your food is pushed along this part of your food tube into your stomach.

... Inside your stomach, your food is broken down by strong juices and turned into a thick, soupy mush.

*.... By now, the useful bits of your food are very tiny. They pass through the sides of the tube and into nearby **blood vessels**.*

.... Any leftover bits of food that your body cannot use are squeezed along to the end of your food tube. You push them out of your body when you go to the toilet.

▼ Babies don't have any teeth to chew their food, so baby food is usually soft and easy to swallow.

◄ Your body is made up mostly of water. Every day, you need to drink fresh water to stay healthy. Your body tells you when to drink by making you feel thirsty.

Quiz Corner

- Why do you need to eat?
- What happens to food in your stomach?
- Which foods give you energy?
- When do you feel thirsty?
- Why is baby food soft?

11

look at: Blood, page 14

Breathing

You need to breathe to stay alive. When you breathe in, you suck air into your body through your nose and mouth. The air goes down a tube in your neck, then into your **lungs**. Your lungs are stretchy bags that fill up with air, in the same way as a sponge fills with water.

▲ When you breathe in, your lungs become bigger as they fill up with air.

Oxygen

In the air around you, there is an invisible gas called **oxygen**. Every time you breathe in, you take oxygen into your lungs. Inside your lungs, oxygen seeps into tubes filled with **blood**. Then your blood carries the oxygen all around your body.

▲ When you breathe out, your lungs become smaller as you push out the air. This air can blow up a balloon.

SEE FOR YOURSELF

When you breathe in, your chest becomes bigger to make room for your lungs. When you breathe out, your chest becomes smaller again. Cross your arms like this and take a deep breath in and out. Can you feel your chest moving?

Breathing out

As your body uses up oxygen, it makes a gas, called **carbon dioxide**. This gas is a **waste** product, which means it is not needed in your body. Your blood carries this gas back to your lungs, so that you can breathe it out. All day and night, you breathe in oxygen and breathe out carbon dioxide.

▼ Fish can breathe underwater, but people cannot. Scuba divers have to carry tanks filled with oxygen on their backs.

Quiz Corner

● What is oxygen?

● How does oxygen get into your body?

● What happens to your chest as you breathe in and out?

● How do divers breathe underwater?

look at: Your muscles, page 8, Eating, page 10, Breathing, page 12

Blood

▼ **Your heart pumps blood around your body.**

Blood is a thick liquid which flows round and round your body. It carries goodness from the food you eat and **oxygen** from the air you breathe to every part of your body. It also picks up **waste** that your body doesn't need and takes it to parts of your body that can get rid of it.

Blood vessels

Blood travels around your body in rubbery pipes called **blood vessels**. These blood vessels run from your **heart** to your **lungs**, then all the way around your body and back again. Sometimes you can see your blood vessels through your skin. They look similar to thin blue lines.

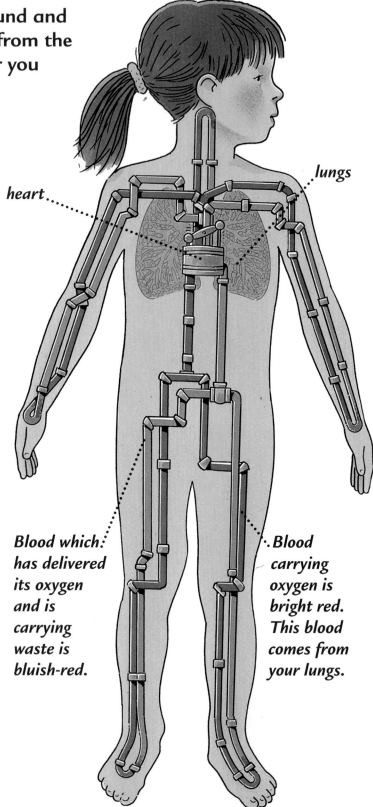

heart

lungs

Blood which has delivered its oxygen and is carrying waste is bluish-red.

Blood carrying oxygen is bright red. This blood comes from your lungs.

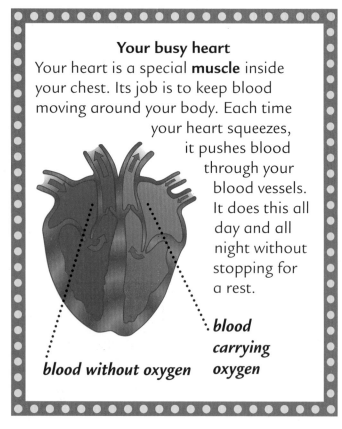

Your busy heart

Your heart is a special **muscle** inside your chest. Its job is to keep blood moving around your body. Each time your heart squeezes, it pushes blood through your blood vessels. It does this all day and all night without stopping for a rest.

blood without oxygen

blood carrying oxygen

New skin

If you cut yourself, thick blood plugs up the hole. Over time, the plug hardens to make a scab. New skin grows under the scab, then the scab falls off.

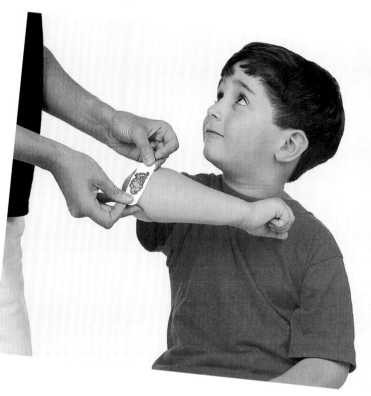

▲ A sticking plaster helps to stop germs getting into your body through a cut. It keeps the cut clean until the skin mends.

CHATTERBOX

If you stretched out all the blood vessels in your body and laid them end to end, they would be almost long enough to go round the Earth three times.

Quiz Corner

● Name three things that blood does.

● What colour is blood with oxygen in it?

● What does your heart do all day and night?

● What happens when you cut yourself?

Fighting germs

Your blood also helps your body to fight **germs**. Germs are tiny living things that can make you sick when they live inside your body. Special **cells** in your blood, called **white blood cells**, fight these harmful germs and help to make you feel well again.

15

look at: Your muscles, page 8, Breathing, page 12, Hearing, page 18, Seeing, page 20, Touching, page 24

Your brain

Inside your head, there is a soft pinky-grey lump protected by your skull. This is your **brain**. Your brain controls your whole body. It tells your **muscles** and **senses** what to do. It also does all your thinking, learning and remembering.

Network of nerves
Your brain is linked to every part of your body by pathways called **nerves**. Your brain sends messages all over your body along these pathways. Different parts of your body also use this network to send messages back to your brain.

CHATTERBOX

The stegosaurus had a very small brain compared with the size of its body. In fact, its brain was the size of a walnut.

▲ This is what the outer layer of your brain looks like. Different parts of your outer brain have different jobs to do.

16

*This part of your brain sends nerve messages to your muscles. It tells them to pull on your **bones** so that you can move.*

This part of your brain controls your speech. It helps you talk to your friends.

This part of your brain receives nerve messages from your eyes. Then it lets you know what you are looking at.

This part of your brain sorts out the nerve messages from your ears. It tells you what you are listening to.

Your brain stem controls things you do which you don't have to think about, such as breathing and sneezing.

Dreams

Your brain works all day and all night. Even when you are asleep, it controls your heartbeat and breathing. Your brain also carries on thinking while you are sleeping. Sometimes you remember these night thoughts as dreams.

▲ Dreams usually last for about half an hour. Most people have about four dreams each night, but don't always remember them.

Quiz Corner

- How long do dreams usually last?
- What does your brain do?
- Your brain is linked to the rest of your body by pathways. What are these pathways called?

look at: Your brain, page 16

Hearing

Hearing is one of your five main **senses**. The others are seeing, smelling, tasting and touching. Your sense of hearing lets you hear many different sounds, from a pin dropping to an elephant trumpeting. It lets you enjoy your favourite music. It can also warn you of many dangers that you cannot see, such as a car speeding up behind you.

Looking at ears

The two flaps on the sides of your head are only part of your ears. The rest of your ears are safe inside your head, covered up by your hard bony skull.

Inside your ears

Your ear flaps are similar to the wide end of a funnel. They catch sounds from the air which go into your ears. In your inner ear, the sounds are turned into messages. These messages whizz along **nerves** to your **brain**. Your brain then tells you what you are listening to.

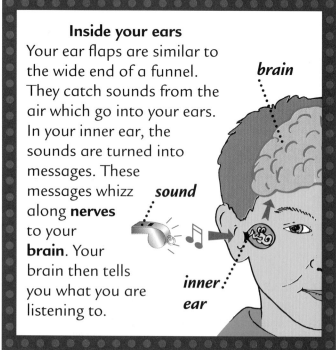

brain

sound

inner ear

▲ Your brain sorts out the sounds you hear. You can tell the difference between the sounds of all kinds of musical instruments.

CHATTERBOX

Many animals can waggle their ear flaps. This means that they can work out where sounds are coming from without turning their heads and attracting enemies.

Silent talk

Often, people who cannot hear learn to talk using special hand signs to spell out and show different words and sentences. This way of talking is called signing.

▲ These children are using signs to talk. The girl is saying that she is tired and the boy wants to know what the time is.

Quiz Corner

● Why is hearing so useful?

● Which part of your body protects your inner ears?

● What can a rabbit do with its ears that you can't?

● How do people who cannot hear talk to each other?

look at: Your brain, page 16

Seeing

Your eyes need light to see. Light bounces off everything you look at and goes into each eye through the small black hole in the middle. Messages about the light are sent along a **nerve** to your **brain** which makes sense of what you see.

▼ Sight is one of your five main **senses**. It gives you a picture of what is happening in the world around you.

20

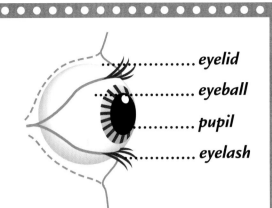

eyelid
eyeball
pupil
eyelash

Eyeball to eyeball
Each of your eyes is similar to a squashy ping pong ball. When you look in the mirror you see only the front of your eyes. The rest of each eye is inside your head.

▼ Some people wear glasses to help them see clearly.

Letting in light
The black hole in the middle of each eye is called the pupil. In dim light, your pupils become bigger to let more light into your eyes. In bright light, your pupils shrink to protect your eyes.

SEE FOR YOURSELF
Ask a friend to stand in a dark room. Look at one of his pupils. Now turn on the light. What do you notice?

Keeping your eyes clean
Salty tears help to keep your eyes clean and wet. You also make tears when you feel unhappy, but nobody knows why.

Wearing glasses
Some people can see things clearly only if they are close by. These people are short-sighted. Others can see things clearly only if they are far away. They are long-sighted. Wearing glasses can help to correct these problems.

Quiz Corner
● What are the black holes in the middle of your eyes called?

● Why do these holes become bigger in dim light?

● What do tears help to do?

● What things can you see clearly if you are short-sighted?

look at: Eating, page 10, Your brain, page 16

Smelling and tasting

Smell and taste are two of your **senses**. When you eat, your tongue picks up tastes and your nose picks up smells. This lets you enjoy the full flavour of your food. Sometimes smells cannot get into your nose because it is blocked by a cold. When this happens, you cannot taste properly.

Inside your nose
Inside your head, the holes leading from your mouth and nose join up. When you eat, smells from your food go up the back of your mouth and into your nose. Inside your nose, smell collectors pick up these smells and send messages about them to your **brain**.

Smells in the air
Your nose doesn't just help your tongue with tasting. It also picks up smells floating in the air around you. Smells are invisible, like the air. When you breathe in, they go up your nose.

▶ Your senses of taste and smell tell you if food is good or bad to eat. Fresh food tastes and smells delicious. Rotten food tastes and smells horrid.

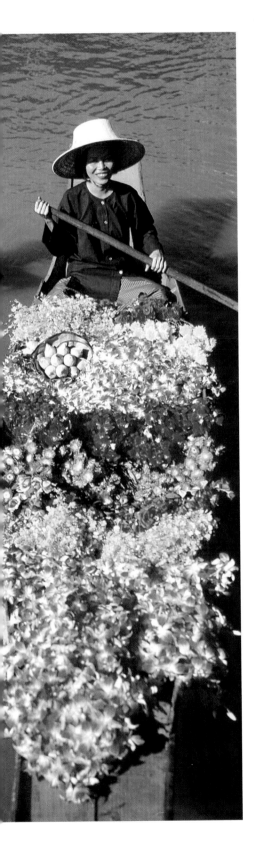

Taste buds

Your tongue is covered in tiny bumps, called taste buds. Taste buds at the front of your tongue pick up sweet and salty flavours. Those on the sides sense sour tastes, such as lemon. Those at the back pick up bitter tastes, such as coffee grains.

This part picks up sour tastes.

This part picks up sweet and salty tastes.

This part picks up bitter tastes.

SEE FOR YOURSELF

Try this test to see how much stronger your sense of smell is than your sense of taste. First blindfold a friend. Now hold an onion under her nose and feed her some bread. What does your friend think she is eating?

Quiz Corner

● Why can't you taste your food properly when your nose is blocked?

● Which four tastes can your taste buds pick up?

● Why are your senses of taste and smell useful?

look at: Your brain, page 16, Skin, page 26

Touching

Your **sense** of touch lets you know how things feel against your skin. When you stroke something with your hand, **nerves** in your skin send messages about the feeling to your **brain**. If the feeling is horrible or unfamiliar, your brain tells you to snatch your hand away. If the feeling is safe and soft, your brain lets you leave your hand where it is.

▶ Stroking the soft fur of a pet is a great feeling. So is giving a cuddle to someone you love.

SEE FOR YOURSELF

Here's a way to test a friend's sense of touch. Make a hole in the side of a box and ask a friend to stick his hand through it. Now put different things, such as cold spaghetti, a potato and a leaf, inside the box. Can your friend guess what each thing is just by touching it?

Different feelings

Your sense of touch tells you if something is hot or cold, hard or soft, rough or smooth. It also lets you know if something is hurting you. Pain is useful because it lets you know when something is harming your body.

▲ Your sense of touch warns you if a drink is hot or cold. It also tells you if things are wet.

▲ When you stand on a drawing pin, a sharp pain tells you to take your foot away.

▲ When you shake hands, you can feel your friend's hand pressing against yours.

◀ A pineapple's skin feels rough and hard, but an apple's skin feels smooth.

Tongue, lips and fingertips

Some parts of your skin feel things more clearly than others because they have more nerve endings. Your fingertips, tongue and lips have lots of nerve endings. This is why a baby often feels things with its mouth.

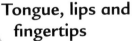

▲ Often, a baby finds out what shape a toy is by putting it in its mouth.

Quiz Corner

● Which part of your body feels things more clearly – the back of your hand or the tips of your fingers?

● Why is pain useful?

● Why does a baby often put things in its mouth?

look at: Touching, page 24

Skin

Your skin is like a stretchy, washable, showerproof suit that covers you from head to toe. It helps stop harmful things from getting into your body. It also works hard to keep you at the right **temperature**.

▶ Your skin stops water soaking into your body. It also stops the inside of your body from drying out in the sun.

Skin colour

Everyone's skin has a kind of dye, or colour, called melanin. Melanin helps to protect skin from the sun's harmful rays. People with dark skin have more melanin than people with fair skin. This means that dark skin is better protected from the sun than fair skin. In sunny weather, skin makes more melanin to protect itself. This is why your skin may become darker in the sun.

Sweat

Your skin is covered in tiny holes called pores. When you are very hot, salty water, called sweat, comes out of the pores. As the sweat dries, it takes heat away from your skin. This helps to cool you down.

CHATTERBOX

Reptiles, such as geckos and snakes, cannot sweat to keep cool. Instead, when they are hot, they have to lie in a shady spot and wait until they cool down.

Save your skin

Too much sunshine can burn and damage your skin. If you want to have fun in the sun safely, follow these rules.

● Wear a wide-brimmed hat to protect your face.

● Use sun cream on any parts of your body not covered up by clothes.

Looking at hair

Hair grows all over your skin, except on your lips, the soles of your feet and the palms of your hands. In some places your hairs are easy to see. In others, they are so tiny, you have to look closely to find them.

▲ The hair on your head grows faster than the hair on the rest of your body.

Having a haircut

The roots of your hair, which are inside your skin, are alive and growing. But the part of your hair that you can see is dead. This is why having a haircut doesn't hurt.

Quiz Corner

● Why do you sweat when you are hot?

● How can you save your skin from sunburn?

● Which part of your hair is alive?

● Where doesn't your hair grow?

look at: Your muscles, page 8, Eating, page 10

Taking care of yourself

There are lots of ways of taking care of yourself. Eating the right food is one way. Getting enough sleep and exercise are other ways. Washing your body, cleaning your teeth and combing your hair each day are important too. This is because keeping clean makes you look, feel and smell good.

Sugar alert

Sugary foods and drinks are great for a treat and give you an instant boost of **energy**. But to keep healthy, you should eat a mixture of all the different types of foods, including plenty of fresh fruit and vegetables.

Grown-up teeth

At about the age of six, you start to lose your first set of teeth. One by one, your second set of teeth grow in their place. You have only one set of grown-up teeth, so make sure you take care of them.

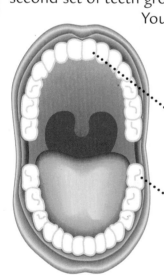

Your front teeth are for biting and tearing food.

Your back teeth are for grinding and chewing food.

28

Keeping happy and healthy

Playing football, going for a walk, running and swimming are all kinds of exercise. Taking exercise regularly helps to keep your body fit and strong. It's good fun too.

Now wash your hands

You should always wash your hands before eating or touching food. This stops any **germs** that might be on your hands from getting on to your food and making you ill.

▲ Playing outside with friends is a good way to exercise.

◀ To wash yourself really well you need to use soap and clean water. The soap loosens the greasy dirt on your skin and the water washes it away.

Quiz Corner

● What can you do to take care of yourself?

● How many sets of teeth do you have in your lifetime?

● Why should you wash your hands before meals?

● How does soap work?

Amazing facts

● The human ear can tell the difference between more than 1,500 different musical sounds.

☆ Every night, you grow a little longer as the discs between the bones in your back stretch. During the day, you shrink back to your usual height.

● Did you know that you blink about 20,000 times a day? Blinking helps to wash dust and germs from your eyes.

☆ Your body sheds tiny flakes of skin all the time. Every year, you shed about 200 grams of dead skin. Most house dust is really made up of dead skin.

● Your hair grows faster in the morning than it does at night.

☆ Did you know that your bones are not made of the strongest material in your body? The tough outer covering on your teeth, called enamel, is stronger.

● The smallest bone in your body is in your ear. It is called the stirrup and is only about the size of a pea!

☆ Inside your head, you have around 14,000 million brain cells. These control everything that your body does.

● A sip of milk takes just six seconds to travel from your mouth to your stomach. Food takes up to 24 hours to pass through your body.

☆ When you sneeze, you force air out of your lungs at a speed of up to 165km per hour. This is faster than a hurricane!

● Did you know that you have the same number of bones in your neck as a giraffe? Seven!

☆ The human body can stay alive for three weeks without food, but only a few minutes without oxygen.

Glossary

blood A thick liquid which flows around your body. Blood is made up of watery fluid, red blood cells and **white blood cells.**

blood vessels Tubes that carry **blood** around the body.

bones The hard white parts inside your body that make up your skeleton.

brain The control centre of your body.

carbon dioxide A **waste** gas your body makes when it uses **oxygen**. Your **blood** carries it to your **lungs** and you breathe it out.

cell A tiny living unit. All living things are made up of cells.

energy The strength to do things.

germ A tiny living thing that can make you sick.

heart The **muscle** that pumps **blood** around your body.

lungs You breathe in and out with your lungs.

muscles Parts inside your body which help move your **bones** and make your food tubes work.

nerves Parts that carry messages to and from your **brain**.

oxygen A gas in the air. Oxygen goes into your **lungs** when you breathe in. Then it passes from your lungs into your **blood** and travels to all parts of your body.

senses The powers which make you aware of the world around you. Your five senses are sight, hearing, touch, smell and taste.

temperature How hot or cold something is.

vitamins and minerals Substances found in food. You need them to keep you healthy.

waste Something your body doesn't need.

white blood cells Parts of your **blood** that destroy **germs**.

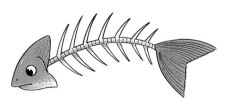

Index

Created by:
Two-Can Publishing Ltd
346 Old Street
London EC1V 9NQ
and Eljay Yildirim of Thunderbolt,
London

Text: Rachel Wright
Consultant: Dr R Ibrahim
Watercolour artwork: Stuart Trotter
Computer artwork: D Oliver
Commissioned photography:
Steve Gorton

© Two-Can Publishing Ltd, 1997

This edition published 1997 by:
Two-Can Publishing
in association with
Franklin Watts
96 Leonard Street
London EC2A 4RH

Hardback ISBN 1-85434-405-6
Dewey Decimal Classification 612

2 4 6 8 10 9 7 5 3 1

A catalogue record for this book is
available from the British Library.

Printed in the USA by
R. R. Donnelley & Sons Co.

Photographic credits: Britstock-IFA
(Weststock, David Perry) p11tr,
(Bernd Ducke) p18-19c; Steve
Gorton p7, p15, p17, p19br, p26,
p27, p28-29c; Images FC; Pictor
International p22-23; Fiona Pragoff
p7, p8-9, p24; Reflections Photo
Library (Jennie Woodcock) p25bl;
Tony Stone Images p4-5, p5, p21,
p29tr; Telegraph Colour Library p20;
Zefa p11c, p13.